AN AUGMENTED REALITY POPUP BOOK

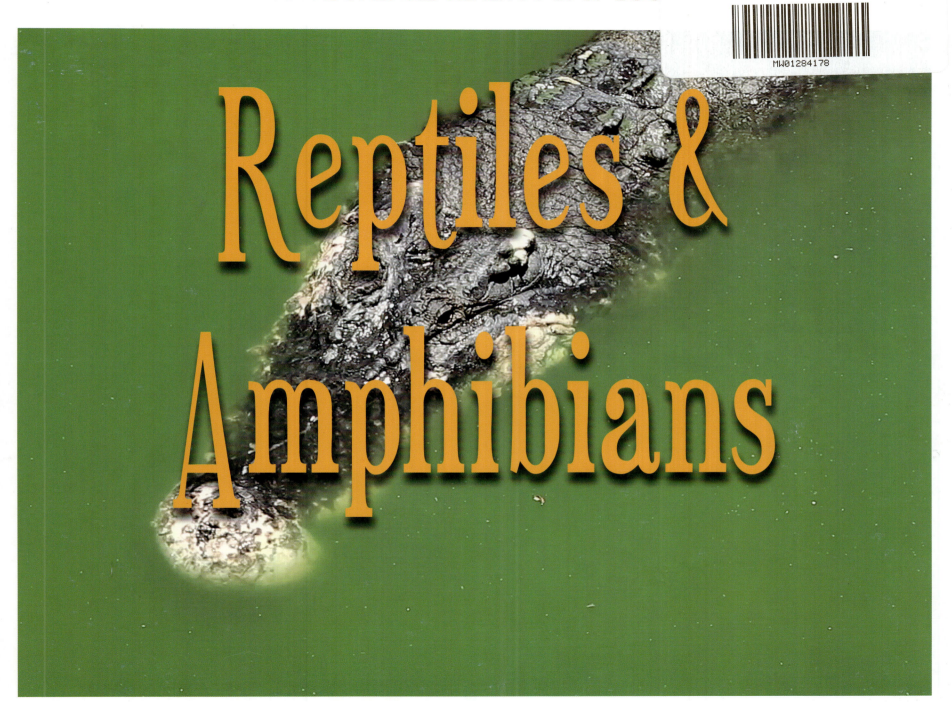

Reptiles & Amphibians

ERNEST KING

Reptiles

The earliest reptiles were believed to be alive over 310 million years ago. Dinosaurs were among those ancient reptiles that roamed the Earth before going extinct. Some of today's living reptiles include snakes, lizards, alligators, crocodiles, turtles, and tortoises. Reptiles live on all the continents except for Antarctica.

All reptiles are cold-blooded. This means they cannot regulate their body temperature. When they get too warm, they go into the shade or the water to cool down. And when they get too cold, they move into the sun to warm up.

All reptiles are covered in scales or have a bony external plate, like a turtle's shell, to protect their body. The scales may be large or small and may be hard or soft.

Reptiles are vertebrates, which means animals with backbones. They breathe air using lungs, and nearly all reptiles lay eggs on land. They are born with very strong instincts, and it's a good thing because most reptiles are left on their own at birth with no parents to watch over them.

The baby sea turtle in the image to the right has just hatched from its shell. Using its natural instincts, the turtle is immediately heading for the water to avoid predators on land. And amazingly, female sea turtles are known to return several years later to the exact beach where they were born to lay their eggs.

Use the mobile app, described on the inside cover, to share the thrill of exploring these wonderful creatures as you discover the pages of this book. The app uses augmented reality to bring every page to life.

A newly born Kemp's ridley sea turtle heads for the water immediately after hatching from its egg.

When this venomous two-striped forest pitviper flicks its tongue out, it is gathering tiny chemical particles from the air. When the tongue goes back into its mouth that chemical information is sent to the brain and quickly analyzed so that the snake can act to avoid predators or catch prey.

Although dinosaurs have been extinct for 65 million years, humans have uncovered fossils and used science to help us understand what dinosaurs looked like and how they moved. Animations like this Tyrannosaurus rex can help us picture a time when dinosaurs roamed the Earth.

Of the meat-eating dinosaurs, Tyrannosaurus rex was one of the largest that ever lived. Standing 15 to 20-feet tall with a length of about 40-feet, the T-rex was at the top of the food chain. The largest T-rex tooth found was 12-inches long. Evidence from fossils indicates that they ate other dinosaurs.

The unique anatomy of the chameleon's eyes gives them the ability to see their environment in nearly 360 degrees. Their eyes can work together or move independently of one another. They can even look forward and backward at the same time!

Like many geckos, this turnip-tailed gecko has no eyelids. Instead, it has a clear scale called a spectacle over its eyes. And since it can't blink, it uses its tongue like a windshield wiper to clean the spectacles. Vertical slit pupils protect geckos from damaging sun rays since they can't close their eyes.

Rattlesnakes are capable of biting and injecting venom - but they would rather be left alone, so they use their rattle to warn potential predators to steer clear. Their rattles are made of keratin, the same material that forms your fingernails. A new rattle segment forms each time a rattlesnake sheds.

This eyelash viper feels right at home in the trees. It's a venomous pit viper species found in Central and South America. Vipers, boas, and pythons have holes in their face called pit organs which allow them to sense heat, enabling them to hunt for prey in complete darkness.

This full-grown dwarf caiman represents the smallest member of the alligator and caiman family, with a maximum length of less than 5 feet. Their small size compared to other crocodilian species has caused some people to seek them as pets, but don't let their size fool you. They can still bite!

Now it's time to meet the largest reptile alive today, the saltwater crocodile! An average-sized male can weigh 1,000 pounds and reach 17 feet long. Specimens weighing over 2,000 pounds and over 20 feet long and have been recorded. They are apex predators (at the top of the food chain).

Anoles are arboreal lizards, meaning they spend most of their time in trees. This Berthold's bush anole is native to tropical Central and South America. Anoles have a dewlap, or flap of skin, hanging from their neck. Males will often puff out their dewlap to attract females or warn outsiders to stay away.

Fire breathing dragons may only exist in myths and fairy tales, but the Komodo dragon is very real. It is the largest lizard in the world, with some weighing over 300 pounds and reaching lengths up to 10 feet. A Komodo dragon is capable of eating 80 percent of its body weight in one meal!

Iguanas have a unique third eye on top of their head called a parietal eye. It doesn't quite see like a normal eye, but it can detect changes in lightness and darkness, allowing this green iguana to munch on a tasty leaf and still watch for potential predators trying to sneak up on it from above.

This chameleon is carefully sneaking up on a grasshopper. It doesn't have to get too close though, as chameleons possess some secret weapons. They have saliva 400 times stickier than human's and a tongue that can quickly extend to twice the length of their body (not including their tail).

To adapt to life in the Galápagos Islands, marine iguanas learned to swim in the ocean and eat algae. They are the only marine lizard species in the world. With such a salty diet, they need to expel the excess salt from their bodies frequently - so they sneeze it out through glands near their nose.

Hawksbill sea turtles earned their name because of their narrow, pointed beak resembling a bird's beak. They primarily feed on sponges, using their beak to extract them from crevices on the coral reef. They also eat jellyfish and sea anemones. Hawksbills are a critically endangered species.

Amphibians

Amphibians are animals that spend part of their lives in water and part on land. There are more than 4,000 different kinds. Frogs, toads, salamanders, newts, and caecilians are all members of the amphibian group. They are cold-blooded vertebrates, like reptiles. But instead of scales, amphibians have moist, thin skin that allows them to breathe and absorb water. To prevent their skin from drying out, they require habitats near water like ponds, swamps or other moist places.

Young amphibians look nothing like their parents. Frogs, for example, begin life as tadpoles with gills to allow them to breathe underwater and tails to help them swim. As they get older, they develop lungs, grow legs, and lose their tail. This process is called metamorphosis.

Since amphibians have permeable skin which takes in water and helps them breathe, they require clean, healthy water. If the water in their habitat is polluted, their health will be affected. For this reason, a reduction in the amphibian population can be an early indicator of problems in an ecosystem.

Amphibians play an important role in their ecosystems, both as predators and as prey. They eat insects, including some that spread disease and damage crops. Amphibians also eat aquatic vegetation and other smaller animals. They will pretty much eat any live creature that they can fit it in their mouth. In an ecosystem that does not include fish, amphibians are often the top predator. But amphibians are also an important food source for their predators, including snakes, birds, fish, mammals, and even other amphibians.

An Amazon leaf frog casually climbing.

This spotted tree frog is waking up in the Amazon Rainforest. Spotted tree frogs can change from this bright yellowish green color in the daytime to dark red at night. Several other types of frogs can also change colors in response to factors like temperature, brightness, or humidity.

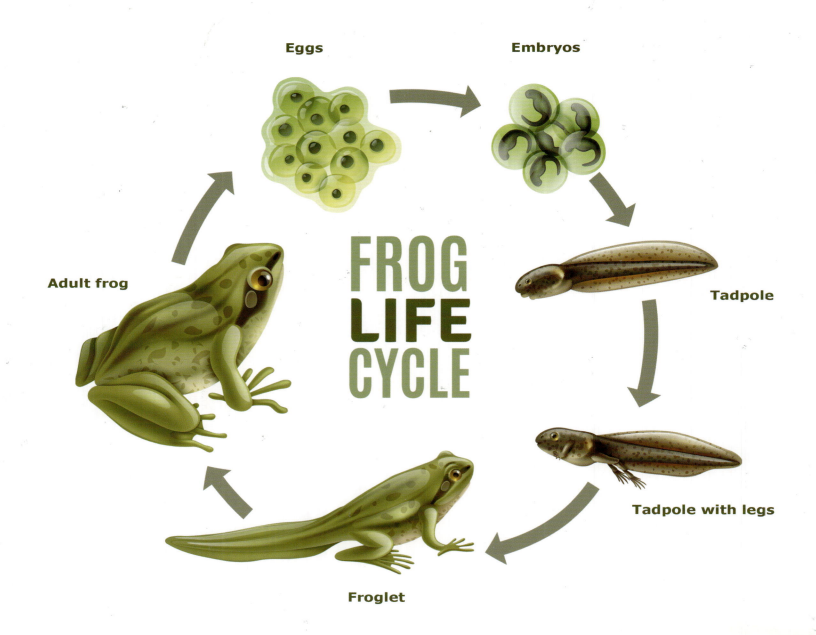

Female frogs lay eggs in masses called a spawn. Tadpoles emerge from the eggs with flat tails for swimming and gills for breathing underwater. They grow hind legs, then front legs. Finally, they develop lungs for breathing air, the tail absorbs into their body, and they are ready to hop on land.

FROG ANATOMY

Internal Organs

Frogs have the same basic organs as humans, including a heart, a brain, lungs, a stomach, a liver, a spleen, kidneys, a small intestine, a large intestine, a pancreas, a gall bladder, and a urinary bladder.

Skeleton

A frog's skeleton, especially their limbs, are similar to a person's. The frog's hind legs include bones called the femur, tibia, and fibula, just like a human's legs. Although the frog's tibia and fibula are fused together making a tibiofibula, which makes jumping easier.

Muscles

In both frogs and humans, the muscles adhere to the skeleton. Humans have a more extensive muscular system, allowing us to perform several various skills, while a frog's muscles are more dedicated to one primary ability: jumping.

Although humans and frogs are very different in outward appearance, we share many similarities in terms of our internal organs, bones, and muscles.

In many ways, frogs and toads are similar, but they also have their differences. Frogs usually live in water like ponds or streams. Toads live on land and can be found in forests, fields, and gardens. Most frogs have moist, slimy skin, while toads, like this crested forest toad, have dry, bumpy skin.

This leaf frog is taking careful aim before quickly leaping to snatch the fly. It takes only a fraction of a second for a frog to roll out its tongue, stick to its prey, and pull it back into its mouth.

A rare species threatened by habitat loss, this Amazon climbing salamander is slowly strolling by. They live in cloud forests in the Andes Mountains of Equador and southern Colombia. A cloud forest is a very moist forest with low and almost constant cloud cover, perfect for amphibians.

It may look like a snake or a giant worm, but this caecilian (pronounced suh-si-lee-uhn) is actually a legless amphibian. Most are less than 6 inches long, but the largest caecilian species can reach lengths up to 5 feet. They have tiny eyes that are only capable of sensing light and dark.

Like all poison dart frogs, these golden poison frogs rely on their bright color to scare off potential predators. This particular species is one of the most toxic animals in the world; a single frog has enough poison to kill ten men. Native hunters once used them to make poison darts.